THE WRONG PERSON TO ASK

Marjorie Lotfi was born in New Orleans, moved to Tehran as a baby with her American mother and Persian father, and fled Iran with one suitcase and an hour's notice during the Iranian Revolution. After waiting with family for her father's return in her mother's tiny hometown in Ohio, she lived in different parts of the US before moving to New York as a young lawyer in 1996 and then back and forth to the UK, settling there in 1999, and in Scotland in 2005. She now lives in Edinburgh.

Her poems have been published in journals and anthologies in the UK and US, including *Staying Human* and *Best Scottish Poems 2021*, and performed on BBC Radio Scotland and BBC Radio 4. Her pamphlet *Refuge*, poems about her childhood in revolutionary Iran, was published by Tapsalteerie Press in 2018. She was one of the three winners of the inaugural James Berry Poetry Prize in 2021, and her first book-length collection, *The Wrong Person to Ask* (Bloodaxe Books, 2023), is a Poetry Book Society Special Commendation.

She has been the Poet in Residence at Jupiter Artland, Spring Fling and the Wigtown Book Festival. She was commissioned to write Pilgrim, a sequence about migration between Iran and the US, for the St Magnus Festival in Orkney, and by the University of Edinburgh to write a European/female/migration counterpart, some of which appears in *The Wrong Person to Ask*.

She founded the Belonging Project, considering the experiences of refugees with over 1,500 participants across Scotland, and is a Co-Founder and Director of the charity Open Book. She is an Ignite Fellow with the Scottish Book Trust, one of the 12 Collective of women writers, co-editor of *New Writing Scotland*, and chair of the board of StAnza, Scotland's International Poetry Festival.

MARJORIE LOTFI

The Wrong Person
to Ask

BLOODAXE BOOKS

ISBN: 978 1 78037 639 4

First published 2023 by
Bloodaxe Books Ltd,
Eastburn,
South Park,
Hexham,
Northumberland NE46 1BS

www.bloodaxebooks.com
For further information about Bloodaxe titles
please visit our website and join our mailing list
or write to the above address for a catalogue.

Supported using public funding by
**ARTS COUNCIL
ENGLAND**

Cover design: Neil Astley & Pamela Robertson-Pearce.

Printed in Great Britain by Bell & Bain Limited, Glasgow, Scotland, on
acid-free paper sourced from mills with FSC chain of custody certification.

for Pete, Nasreen, Florence and John,
who will always be home to me

CONTENTS

I

13 Refuge

14 On seeing Iran in the news, I want to say

15 The Wrong Person to Ask

16 Two Grandmothers

17 Maman Bozorg

18 The gun in its holster

19 Riding the Line

20 The Game

21 Crossing the street for mother's cigarettes

22 Shut Out the Noise

23 Packing for America

24 Hope

25 To the Airport

26 Origin

27 The Last Thing

28 Alarm I

29 Alarm II

30 I Picture of Girl and Small Boy (Burij, Gaza, 2014)

31 II Picture of Boy, Looking Away (Gaza, 2015)

32 Gabriella's Dream

33 What You See in the Dark

34 Wishbone

35 Correction

36 Destruction of the Forty Martyrs Cathedral, Aleppo, Syria

37 Granddaughter, I entered your mother's house

38 Checkpoint, Matveyev Kurgan

39 Khanoom

40 The End of the Road

40   I [There's a moment every morning]

41   II [Each breath in this place]

42   III [Every blade against the cutting-board]

43   IV [She takes her boys back every summer]

44   V [Even in this lack of light, she sees]

45   VI [The boys carry her good looks]

46   VII [In her eightieth year, she sees her sisters]

II

49   Sea Gooseberry *(Pleurobrachia)*

50   Sunday on the Luing Sound

51   Number 9 Cullipool

52   Sunflower

53   Star of the Sea

54   Williamina Fleming

55   What Work Is

56   Omega Centauri

57   Drift

58   Say It's Nothing, Say It's Rust

59   Horizon

60   Out to Sea

61   When They Ask

62   The Trunk

63   After the Match

64   The first thing he doesn't forget

65   The Unfinished House

66   Storm Light

67   The Last Keeper

68   Citizen

69   Moving

70   And this is how it begins

71   O Love!

72   Edward Thomas on His Last Night with Helen

73   Keep

74   The Hebridean Crab Apple

76   ACKNOWLEDGEMENTS

Prayer

Give me a little less
with every dawn:
colour, a breath of wind,
the perfection of shadows,

till what I find, I find
because it's there,
gold in the seams of my hands
and the night light, burning.

JOHN BURNSIDE

I

Refuge

after 'Les Voyageurs', sculptures with large portions
of their bodies missing, by Frances Bruno Catalano

Take out his heart,
lungs, one arm, the whole
belly, and the belt strap
that holds it all in place.
Let the lighthouse beacon
throw its false light
through him, promise
safe passage. Take out
his thighs, but leave
his knees to buckle
at kindness, and the lack
of it. Don't loosen his grip
on the suitcase; it holds
all he owns. Instead, nail
his feet to the planks
of the pier and let him try
to take another step.

On seeing Iran in the news, I want to say

my grandmother was called Nasreen,
that she died two years ago in Tabriz
and I couldn't go to say goodbye,
that she knew nothing of power,
nuclear or otherwise. I want to say
that the bonfires for *Chahar Shanbeh Suri*
were built by our neighbour's hands;
as children we were taught to jump over
and not be caught by the flames. I want to say
my cousin Elnaz, the one born after I left,
has a son and two degrees in Chemistry,
and had trouble getting a job. I want to say
that the night we swam towards
the moon hanging over the horizon
of the Caspian Sea, we found ourselves
kneeling on a sandbar we couldn't see
like a last gift. I want to say
I'm the wrong person to ask.

The Wrong Person to Ask

Ask me for the measure of rose water
in baklava, how to butter each layer of filo
away from the corner so it holds itself
apart under heat, or the exact crush
of pistachio, fine as rubble, not yet dust.

Ask why the man squatting on our roof
in the worst sun of Ramadan refused even a sip
of my water. *Hitchi*, he'd said, *I want nothing.*
Ask me how to speak one kind of English
at school and another at home.

Ask about the cherry tree at the bottom
of the garden, and the only time I remember it
in fruit: my father smiling, pulling me
from the cleft of its branches in darkness.
Ask about the bars on my bedroom window.

Ask me how many sugar cubes I could slip into
my chai before Maman Bozorg noticed. (Four.)
Ask me how to *taarof*, to say no when you mean
yes. Ask about the army of ants, daytimes,
and cockroaches, nights, how they fly into dreams.

Ask how the grandfather clock of a samovar,
its bubble and hiss, marks out time in the house.
Ask about Ameh, her arms around my skinny frame,
or how I can have forgotten Farsi and the sound
of her voice bidding me each night to let the day go.

Two Grandmothers

Tehran, 1978

The old woman from Tabriz, dark floral chador,
sits at her only table, bought for this meeting.

She speaks no English but speaks; tells stories
in Farsi, a second language she learned at school.

The other old woman from Frankfort, Ohio,
isn't listening. She's taking in Tehran like the lights

of her first Ferris wheel at the Ross County Fair;
the twinkling against night sky almost blinding,

so other. The first woman understands.
In the small tick of tongue against the roof

of a mouth – *no, cut it out, I don't agree* – or
the slow blink of eyelids – *yes, okay, you're right* –

meaning can be mistaken. She reaches up inside
swathes of black, nudges down two gold bangles,

a wedding gift, each as thin as wire or a cord
to tie an old gate shut. She takes the hand

of the strange American turning it upwards,
opens out each long finger and places her bangles

into that pink palm, insisting; a gift.
Gabel nadare, she says – *it's nothing.*

Maman Bozorg

It doesn't matter that she's blonde,
this new daughter-in-law, doesn't know
a word of Farsi, or how to *taarof*, always
refuse first, before accepting a gift.

What you believe is your own trouble;
not one of us understands all the words
of our mother tongue. 'Look at the eye,'
my father told me, 'watch it speak.'

As long as you are here, I will be shelter,
will walk the length of my own bazaar
and ask the jeweller to sell me a crucifix,
give it to you with these heavy words.

Believe in something: your hands pressed
together, palm to palm, are my body folded
into the *namaz*; each of us maps ourselves
in the mirror, measures what we already know.

The gun in its holster

like a rifle leant against a tree
in a winter wood, is just waiting
to go off. Look closely: decoy paisley
adorns the inlay, and one tear-shaped
dropper points a warning
from the sidelock. When held,
the trigger needs no convincing,
no embellishment, is as familiar
as the handle of that old
hunting knife handed
down from your father
as your great-grandfather's
one good thing.

Riding the Line

on the cusp of the Iranian Revolution, Tehran, 1978

When Uncle Siavush takes Kamran out for a ride,
only three years between them, their skateboarding
the usual teenaged pastime, the Shah's guards look on,
unsmiling, remembering their boards at home.

The boys watch the pavement: the fissures, cracks,
and the men line the road behind mirrored sunglasses,
their guns slung backwards; like children in rucksacks,
they want to join in. They ride the block for three long hours.

Silent, waiting, Maman Bozorg (both mother and grandmother)
rocks her outstretched legs with her eyes shut; no baby at home
to bed. The boys put their skateboards away in the cupboard,
kneel on the carpet to supper; nothing broken, nothing said.

The Game

There was the game of counting
        gunshots in a riot,
and buying cigarettes
        for our too-blonde mother;
the game of the school set on fire
        while we were still in it,
and watching the clock until
        the return of my brother.

There was the game of one toy
        for the journey,
of taking my lunchbox
        and filling it instead;
the game of hiding mother
        on the way to the airport,
father at the barrier
        while we went ahead.

There was the game of turning
        your ring inwards,
giving it to the man at the gate
        to let you pass;
the game of finding your seat
        on the flight,
eyeing those in the aisles
        who got on last.

Crossing the street for mother's cigarettes

(she is blonde, she is American)
to the shop a block from home.
I skip over shrapnel, the vestige
of last night: the curfew and blackout,
a clash I heard through my window,
and wonder at the constitution
of puddles: water, gasoline, blood?
I have been taught to cross this road –
busy with traffic – with care.
Tehran drivers don't watch
for small children. But this morning,
the road is silent. I cross it, first looking
both ways, then again – half expecting,
half willing those cars I can almost
still hear to reappear.

Shut Out the Noise

Close your eyes, cup your hands
over your ears, then speak. Say
the day they shot all the doctors
at the hospital for refusing to hide
bodies, I was the girl watching
from her grandmother's rooftop. Say
the staccato of sniper fire
was a call to prayer,
and the nightly track of tanks
a low toll of bell, more pressure
of sound than sound itself. Say
the fire at our school was set or
the man dressed in white robes
walking our blacked-out road
after curfew asked a question
without opening his mouth. Say
the words on every brick
hurtled through our window:
Yankee go home.

Packing for America

my father in Tabriz, 1960

He can't take his mother in the suitcase,
the smell of *khoresht* in the air, her spice box
too tall to fit. Nor will it close when he folds
her *sajadah* into its corners. He can't bring
the way she rose and blew out the candles
at supper's end, rolled up the oilcloth, marked
the laying out of beds, the beginning of night.
He knows the slap of her sandals across
the tiles will fade. He tosses photographs
into the case, though not one shows her eyes;
instead, she covers her mouth with her hand
as taught, looks away. He considers strapping
the samovar to his back like a child's bag;
a lifetime measured in tea from its belly.
Finally, he takes her tulip glass, winds
a chador around its body, leaves the gold rim
peeking out like a mouth that might
tell him where to go, what is coming next.

Hope

Strip it off, along with boots,
the silver buckled belt and a bag,
too small, of your possessions.

Carry only your children. Cut
your hair. Throw loose change
and glasses overboard.

Curl into a child's pose, spine
aligned with spine, to form a human
keel. Cling to the other side.

To the Airport

Tehran, 11 December 1978

She wraps a black scarf
          around her white face
the way her mother-in-law   has shown her
          when the car edges   towards Shayad Square

(do not look into the eyes of men)

No voices   just a roar   no birdsong
          but gunfire in winter sunlight
this the mother   of all riots

She slouches down   the well of leather seats
          diminishing   her height
a dead giveaway

(speak only Farsi)

Kamran   her boy   already tall beside her
          knows   they aren't coming back
his fingers gripping her leg like a toddler
          still   he blocks the view
the streets   full   guards
          protesters   her English students

(lower your eyes to hide their colour)

Her hands   layered with rings
          one hand   slipped under her thigh
the other   held by Bahman her husband
          this rare gesture   his goodbye

Origin

She tends the two lights – left and right –
of her headlamps, doesn't care for newsprint
or radio, reports of blazes, the world on fire.
She can't see the end, which house will be
her last, or which county, country.
She doesn't think about endings but light,
worries the cocoon of glass-like plastic
will crack open under the weight of a stone
or an animal's skull, one slow black wing.
She doesn't tend what's behind,
refuses to look in the rear-view mirror
with its clarity of black and white.
She lets the red lamps of hindsight
burn out on a road she's already
forgotten. The car is a womb and she
is unborn. *Where are you from?*
people ask. She refuses to say.

The Last Thing

a boy throws his coat overboard in Sergey Ponomarev's
Pulitzer Prize-winning image of migrants landing in Greece

She always told him to put his coat on,
but he didn't feel the cold. Nights
he'd come home without it, to be sent
back out for its black form waiting
like a dead animal on the corner
where the only streetlamp still worked,
where football was possible after dark.
The morning he leaves, she pushes it
into his bag like a relic, listing the reasons
he'll need the weight, winter is coming.
It's the last thing he loses. When all the bags
are gone and the men chest-deep
in water hauling the boat to land, he keeps
his shoes for shore, flings the coat overboard.

Alarm I

Tehran, 1978

Our fifteen small heads bow
as if in prayer, arms at an angle,
wrestling the unfamiliar loop
and curve, right to left, of Farsi
when the first siren rings
like a mourner's wail. Suddenly,
each of us knows this Revolution,
its pyre quietly built in the corner
of sight, and all we'd done to set it
alight was open our mouths.
Our teacher climbs on a desk,
points at the door; her voice
steadies as we file out
to the smoky playground
and wait for whatever
will happen next.

Alarm II

Washington DC, 1983

Now the Russians: the sound
of the siren changes, not the bell
for recess or the fire drill
but a drone dragging on the brain,
two discordant notes playing
on and on without pause.

Rising in unison, we count out
of the room in alphabetical order
to the sixth-grade spot in the hallway,
face the wall and drop to our knees
like folding onto a prayer mat. Each
of us freezes in the brace position.

We live through fire, and years
later practise our safe escape,
before the Principal announces
on the loudspeaker in every class
that today's exercise was only
a drill, that we'd done it well.

I Picture of Girl and Small Boy (Burij, Gaza, 2014)

I would like to tell her not to wear such flimsy shoes,
that rubble contains the whole spectrum of knowable
and unknowable dangers: sheets of metal, ripped
to knife edge, live wires, bloated arms reaching

for light. Her hair, scraped back into a ponytail,
is open to sky; remnants of buildings filter down
one concrete chunk at a time, and the midday bells
of rockets ring out above her. She carries a boy

on her still narrow hips, his legs entwined around
her yellow dungarees. Like a rodeo rider, his left arm
grips her shoulder to steady himself, or her,
while his torso reels back and away; his body

is asking to slow down, to turn back. Instead,
her eyes comb the ground for a next step, fingers
of her free hand curled into a claw, as if
to frighten off what she somehow sees ahead.

II Picture of Boy, Looking Away (Gaza, 2015)

after an image of twelve year-old Abdulrahman, seated on the rubble
of his home where his father (who was also his teacher) was killed by a bomb

I would like to tell the boy to look us in the eye, the cameraman
can do nothing with this angle, that what's left is just more
of the rubble of home he's sitting on like the king

of a demolished kingdom. Around him, sheets of metal coil
under the objects they once sheltered: desk legs, window frames,
still half-open, and the innards of concrete, steel nets poking

from the sand, catching only wind. His knuckles rest
between mouth and nose in a classic thinker's pose,
while the other hand is poised on his hip, fingers bent back

by an invisible bully. If only he had a treasure hidden
behind him, some relic he could offer us now. We don't want
to see that other child at the edge of the frame, or his fist;

instead, we're waiting for the boy to square his gaze
and ask again, *who's going to teach me now?* or hold up
his wrists to the camera, and cry *mercy, mercy.*

Gabriella's Dream

for Gabriella Ratcliffe, and her mother Nazanin Zaghari-Ratcliffe

Every sound in this strange city a sign of the lost:
the footsteps on the stair a different gait, lighter
each night, not just Baba coming up to kiss the air
above her head. Every morning the clatter of shutters
from the shop below becomes the brakes
of a vehicle stopping at their door. Every note
of birdsong her mother's voice saying her name,
that little she can remember. Every promise

Maman Bozorg's tall tale last thing at night:
the wind is a two-armed giant reaching
from the heart of this lit street to Tehran's
barred edges. Every petal and feather she tosses
into its current a code, every barred window
left open in the dark an ear listening to the night.

What You See in the Dark

The missed dipper, smaller, named after
your younger self, not looked for
and not seen since, burning bright

The furrowed fields of an Ohio winter
out the back window, the soil open
to air, waiting for the drill

And each child you lost, as unnamed
and unformed as sea glass: polished, opaque
as light, only clear in watery dreams

Getting out of the city again, the school
on fire, the walled blaze of road,
open fists across the windscreen

Every life you could have lived
dividing, subdividing:

> *you there*, hijabed and waiting for language
> *you there*, foreigner, brown as the soil
> *you there*, a keeper of words
> *you there*, a stranger to yourself, awake in the night

Wishbone

In a Glasgow high-rise, a woman steadies
       a bird in her hands: felted yellow above
the fork of wishbone and emerald at the belly.
       With each hidden stitch she draws the body
into itself. It's not the red-breasted robin
       that lasted the winter on kitchen scraps
or even her brown fledgling, but a bird
       of her own making, taken from an old hijab
and the scraps of tartan her boy brought home
       from school on St Andrew's day. He doesn't want
this half-finished bird she carries folded
       into her chador but the bottle-green parrot
squawking in the pet shop window;
       the one that waits for the boy to come,
holds out its clipped feathers to the light.

Correction

after a photo of the Iranian Revolution, by Kaveh Golestan

The picture she is holding is of the dance –
hundreds of unarmed men moving
at the same time, standing apart.
One holds a bottle aloft – hailing

his fortune – and a boy as tall
as her own could be bowling
that stone from his clenched hand,
the windmill a perfect action, the line

unbroken through the elbow.
She takes a bottle of correction fluid
to the picture, chooses the man
who looks most guilty and paints

him out. Her fingers slip and the liquid
touches a second man, so she begins
on him, the edges of his body blurred,
harder to see. His arm is linked

through that of a third, so he has to
go too, though he looks like he carries
no blame, is just standing watching.
When she's finished, all the men

are gone. Only the forest is left,
the branches of trees bared to the fire,
and a solitary boy playing on his own,
caught in the act of throwing a stone.

Destruction of the Forty Martyrs Cathedral, Aleppo, Syria

for Hrair, who was taken there as a child by his grandfather

As if communication were still possible,
>   the telephone poles stand, wires
strung from shoulder to shoulder.
>   The spire's cross has tilted into a raven,
wings open, preparing for flight. Maybe
>   the bells will ring, one slow shudder
after another, pronounce this death
>   a wedding, the marriage between
what we will to happen, and what will be.

>   Now there is no Last Judgement.
Your grandfather can't lead you
>   to the *khachkar* in the churchyard,
teach you to pray for the dead or conjure
>   the old house, your father's childhood,
over the adjoining wall; you must sift
>   this soft rubble alone, hands bared
to its dangers, and make your own use
>   of what remains.

Granddaughter, I entered your mother's house

as I entered every house, head covered, shoes off.
I wore a black chador for all my outings.
Your mother said *black is for funerals*.
What she didn't know was that I agreed.
This funeral of a life; I'd been in mourning
since my wedding. I entered my son's house
as a stranger, reading each carpet as I might
almond trees in bloom or bolts of cloth
to determine yield, how much they might fetch.
Your parents prospered, didn't always smile.

I placed my shoes at the front door, as is only
proper. *Bebakhshid*, they said. *Beshin eenja*,
pointing to the largest lounge chair. I wanted
to drop to the ground, fold my heels beneath me.
I wanted to speak in the old language, the one
your mother hadn't learned. But instead, I sank
into the seat with a flick of the head, saying
khayli mamnoon, as if grateful, remembering
how hard it is in this foreign land to keep
holding the spine straight, to keep looking down.

Checkpoint, Matveyev Kurgan

for Marina

When her sister moved across the border
there was no border, not even a line
like the one they'd drawn in chalk

down the centre of their bedroom,
dividing walls and window, the light
parsed out between them as if

halving a parent's love. Only the door,
its point of entry and exit, was shared.
And when their own children were born

they passed through checkpoints
on Sundays, not thinking of them
as lines, or points on a map,

but as traffic signals or a low bridge
that never closed, even in high wind.
Now, in the still of ceasefire,

she finds there's no suspension left;
she drives to the edge of no man's land,
flings one arm over to the other side

the way she did as a girl just before
sleep, willing her sister to wake,
to clasp her hand and hold it.

Khanoom

I am not interested in Bolsheviks.
Instead, it's the way light fell
across my daughter's sleeping face,
how she ate pomegranate, mouth brimming
with tiny jewels, the way her nostrils
would flare at the sight of mulberries,
but when offered, *taarofing*, she'd eat.

Like swallows, we migrate,
but there's no spring and no autumn
in this place. Along with the samovar
and the *janamaz*, I was walked
from Baku across the border,
150 miles, a distance I measured
in the steps it would take to return.

Now in Tabriz, my grandson skips
into the courtyard where I spend
daylight wearing a path around
the lilting fountain, speaking to the birds.
He sits next to me under the mulberry tree
and listens before asking if he
can send a message back home, too.

The End of the Road

I

There's a moment every morning
when she forgets – opens her mouth
to her mother tongue and finds
the silence foreign. She feigns sleep,
takes time to replay clips of childhood –
as if donning daily armour – before
opening her eyes. She sees the other girls
on the beach, their laughter ordinary
as birdsong, plots the spring wildflower
and symbols carved on limbs of trees,
pictures the glances across a schoolroom
understood from a lifetime of knowing.
And only then does she rise, carrying
an image of the girls nodding beneath
her eyelids, approving of this version
of her life every time she blinks.

II

Each breath in this place
                is on purpose, every rain-filled hour
a block of time she has chosen
                to square and plant her feet
into this world. She speaks only
                through the tunnel of her language.
At once she is, and never will be,
                one of them. She tends
a shoebox garden on the inside
                of the kitchen window, keeps
the heat on all day, embraces
                a coal fire. She cultivates earnestness,
only speaks truth about the weather.
                She will never understand
daytime soaps or late-night sitcoms.
                On feast days, she pretends
that her sisters will arrive
                to bore the children with toasts,
the correct ordering of dishes.
                In the night she worries
about where her sons will bury
                her body when she is gone.

III

Every blade against the cutting-board
saws her life in half, until she's smaller
and smaller, only fragments of herself.
She grates lemons for zest and strips

rosemary against its spine to remind
herself of the heat required to create life
from a parched and stony earth.
She refuses to be thrifty, bins

the ends of supermarket bread
and buries the smallest cloves
of garlic in the garden rather
than peel their skins. She waits

in spring for the green shoots
to come, the miracle of something
growing from inattention, from
this sliver of almost nothing, ignored.

IV

She takes her boys back every summer.
They stand together, a mute herd, and shift
their feet in the dust as she speaks:

There, she says,

there —

     is the place I buried the doll
in her Sunday clothes, one broken limb
on the earth to mark it,

there —

     is my footbridge over the brook,
the watermelon-sized stones loosed
from mud before the spring tide,

there —

     is the path that led to the old tree,
a yellow ribbon around its branch
for memory, straight as an arrow,

there —

     is the tree's trunk, split by lightning,
the one I'd pulled along the village path
for a place to stop, to rest my feet,

there —

     is the end of the road, the mountain
of hill where my white house stood,
still stands, on its stone foundations.

V

Even in this lack of light she sees
her mother at the window, one hand
on a hidden hip, looking beyond

the kitchen. Even here, in her room,
a sea of water and years between them,
her mother stands and looks out,

less hidden now about her worn
hopes or what little she has retained
in this family of women.

Leave home, she hears her mother
whisper over her sleeping body,
it's not too late.

VI

The boys carry her good looks –
copper skin and blue-black hair –
but more, her grandfather's
green eyes, his trick of laughing
without motion, without a single
crease at the corner of the eyes.

The boys carry her obsession
with the uncharted: desert maps
and sea graphs adorn their walls,
wax-stoppered bottles under
their beds wait to be cast off
into a receding tide.

The boys carry her reverence
for sky; count the constellations
through their window before sleep,
and wake at midnight hoping
for one star more before
the white cloud of daylight.

The boys carry her body, even
while pinning her to this place;
she watches them roll the sea maps
tight against their lengthening
bodies, lift their anchors in slow
motion, prepare to set sail.

VII

In her eightieth year, she sees her sisters
everywhere: the stand of trees at the end
of the garden, the tallest, middle three

huddled together as if keeping a secret,
the last off in a world of her own; their bodies
as girls, bunched up for Papa's night stories,

like the roll of waves in the sea. Even the toes
of her youngest grandchild, peas
in a pod she calls them, recall siblings

in a narrow bed. In her eightieth year,
she stops hearing her mother's voice,
how she sang only when she thought

she was alone, and Papa's laugh –
its burst of ascending notes – in bird call
or wind. In her eightieth year, she returns

to sleeping on the floor, the wood a relief,
straightening her spine. In her eightieth year,
she imagines each sip of tea as home,

searing and black in the old way, sugar held
on the tongue, sweetening what is to come,
what fire in her mouth she has yet to swallow.

II

Sea Gooseberry *(Pleurobrachia)*

Its globe of water is an optical illusion
held in the body of a rock pool, nudging
the arms of a pink anemone, as if wanting
reassurance that the tide will rise, its horizon
of imprisonment will shift. She recognises
the child she's lost, the line between them
still frail as this gelatine edge: diffusing
seawater, barely holding the boundary of self.
She lifts the glistening form into her hand
and then, because she can, she puts it back.

Sunday on the Luing Sound

All day the sailboats have been languorous
        in their gliding between Belnahua –
its quarry denuded, deep water nursing cuttings,
        anchoring this ring of island and its roofless
slate cottages to seawater, one mile offshore –
        and the Fladda Lighthouse, its walled garden
sheltering brambles, the common *twayblade*,
        its two keeper's cottages standing empty,
a colony of terns chattering at closed doors,
        the tall white mast a watchtower reporting *No Danger.*

White sails blow taut like the corners of hospital sheets,
        each gust a snap, a reminder to be grateful,
the sun bleaching blue water and blue air into white.
        Then the fisherman's seiner speeds past,
engine gunning, a running mackerel, dark greens
        of work above, its iridescent belly barnacled
below the surface, hand-tied buoys flailing in wind
        like a fistful of carnival balloons.
Its silver hull flashes through froth,
        hugs the shoreline, heads for home.

Number 9 Cullipool

Mostly he fishes the common lobster,
Homarus gammarus, blue black
as ink or the night sky, speckled
with points of white. He soaks each trap
before setting and baiting it
with the rot of last week's mackerel
salted to stitch its flesh, hold off
the crabs; later, he'll check the parlour
for callers, freeing the odd wrasse or pollack
before nosing his seiner for home.

In season, he takes the clammer out
for scallops, their jellied muscles
as prized as opals, wobbling with fire.
He collects the perfect shells
for his wife, tying them into a swollen string
of fisherman's pearls for her hands to finger
while he's gone. Every morning
as he sets off for the dock, he says
If you find yourself in the sea,
too much has already gone wrong.

Sunflower

Her grandfather had always said
that everything she'd need
was beneath the grey of its shell;
the signposts of winter would come
from its height, the strength of its spine,
how long it resisted before nodding
its head to wind. When she left,

she took nothing but the seeds,
their rattle in the tiny tin better than
money. Now, she sleeps with them
under her pillow where they grow
into her dreams, stakes to lean against
on each crossing, and wakes looking for
yellow petals tangled in her hair.

Star of the Sea

Some miracles take the form of instinct:
the way breath continues when the mind

is gone, how we run from danger or the body
prepares to fight it. That day Father Patrick

took us to the beach to pray, we stood,
not at sea's edge, but away from the water

seeping its way towards our feet. As we prayed
for the souls at sea, each of us was also praying

that a wave wouldn't take us while our eyes
were shut. We all heard the shout for help,

but only Father went into the water.
Once he'd hauled the boy in, his older body

dropped to sand, and we laid our coats
over him until he came to – shouting that he

couldn't have saved anyone, frightened
of water as he was, not being able to swim.

Williamina Fleming

1857–1911, Harvard College Observatory astronomer from Dundee

Tell me every day will ring
like a bell, that the only fog
will be the cloud on a plate,
the low-lying haar of the still
unknown, unseen. Tell me
every sunrise will bring
this knowing: that what is visible
is first visible only to me.
Tell me there are places
beyond sight. (I do not mean
the stars.) Tell me the stramash
of home will settle like a graveyard
by year's end, the sharp spring
will trace new patterns across
this view of the sky I've always
known. Tell me that the sheets
of Scottish rain keep coming,
that I could be that woman
running out to heave in
a damp line of linen.

What Work Is

for Kamran

The closest I ever got to your kind of work
was mowing lawns the summer
my brother spent in California, his knees
scraping sand on the volleyball court,

while I knelt to empty the mower's bucket.
My only job was to keep his jobs going
until he got back, to pocket the bills left
in sheds and under pot plants

or collect them on early evening rounds
like an old woman strolling the neighbourhood
before sundown. When the owners returned
from work to find a girl at the front door,

I watched for that look of surprise;
I waited for the *good for you, honey*.

Omega Centauri

He nudges her arm, holds her chin
between his hands, whispers *Love,*
there's something I need to show you.
Every time she wakes, it's to a hope
he'll reach into his ribcage
and rake it open, unearth his heart.
But every night it's the same:
the telescope dumb in the corner,
its dark sky beyond the window
and lights flickering out of sight,
he says, if only she'll believe.

Drift

after Silvana McLean

When her husband asks her for a self-portrait,
    she paints a watercolour of seaweed, as long
as her body, edges shredded from too much
    beating against rock, refusing to fight the tide.
Tiny barnacles cling to its surface.

He sees pinpricks of light, hangs it on the wall.
    She keeps the piece of seaweed in her studio.
It shrinks to the length of her forearm,
    so she stitches its translucent ends together,
wears it as a cuff around her wrist.

Say It's Nothing, Say It's Rust

after Georgi Gill

The way a bicycle chain goes, say, in rain
or the dent in the fender of a car left
to its own devices, the marriage
is the old blood red of rust, long done
coursing through, delivering what is needed
to the body, long done refreshing.
And when I finally sandpaper it down
against the grain I find the carcass
has worn clean through, a gap large enough
for a fist, two fists, both of them mine.

The way air on the warmest day
of summer forms a mist only we know
as haar, how cloud moves in at the speed
of sound; between us no signal, this nothing
holds until no beacon can penetrate.
So when the weather clears, the shape
of the hills and valleys of years
opens behind us, you emerge, blinking
in the light to say it was nothing,
that the storm was nothing at all.

Horizon

after John Glenday

Imagine it in her hands – because the road does not wind,
the wheel heats beneath her skin; fingertips
imprint the leather in an account of the afternoon.
The world moves in a blur of barriers and leafless trees.

Beside her a girl who looks exactly like her and not
like her – the wave of eyebrow and cocked chin,
a single rope of hair. She refuses to agree on anything
other than the time, the silence between them.

Out to Sea

All week they've been hoarding the useless:
       the length of rope from a trap left out
          like an animal carcass in rain,
packets of sweets wrapped in squares of parchment
       bought at the post office that doubles as a shop,
          the old torch of one fastidious mother
stowed in a hall cupboard ready for a dark night
       and shreds of tobacco stolen from a Grandfather's tin,
          twisted into scraps of last week's paper.
The boat is chosen, not by its size, but by the father –
       the one who sits in the kitchen in his faded dungarees,
          working a cigarette from the break of light,
clutching a picture of himself, once, at sea, looking away –
       and all the boys agree it's the right boat
          without having to say why.
When they drag the hull into the water on the grey shale beach,
       laughter trailing behind with the last of the daylight,
          they're already seasick with delight, pulling oars
through the Luing sound, ducking the Fladda lighthouse beacon,
       aiming to skip slate into the green of the Belnahua quarry
          which floats like a life ring, flung out to sea.

When They Ask

for Nasreen and Florence

She wonders what to tell
her daughters when they ask
for her best hour. *Now*, she wants
to say, *just now*, but instead

tells them about her first
Martini, how she was unsure
whether to lift from the rim
or stem, and afterwards throwing

open her arms to the constellations –
Orion and the backwards Taurus
and Gemini – on the ceiling
of Grand Central Station.

She warns them never to trust
a city clock, to always carry
house keys in a front pocket,
and then adds how walking

the streets of a town where no one
knows your name can itself
be a form of comfort, says
There is safety in loneliness.

The Trunk

Finally, when there is nothing left in the trunk,
her clothing parsed out amongst siblings and cousins
in moments of common sense, she leaves its lid open
so the scent of the child will fade, so she won't be tempted
to put her head inside that box to breathe.
Then she paints the room, chooses the child's favourite
grass green, but can only manage one coat. The cracks
in the tongue and groove glare. She stamps a hole
in the suitcase. But she can't change the bedding;
its grey blankets convey the child's limbs. If only,
like tea leaves in a china cup, she'd read the shape
of the pillows that morning and barred the door.
Now, she knows their pattern, closes her eyes
to see them, crumpled, with a space for her head.

After the Match

'Like a blind man, in a dark room, looking for a black cat that isn't there'
— David Cameron's 2011 description of the campaign for justice
by family members of the victims of the Hillsborough disaster

But the dark is not dark
to the blind, only more
of the same, the way
the dead boy is never
dead to his mother,

just absent another day.
She hears him evening
after evening, coming back
to the flat, late home
from the match, shuffling

slowly between rooms
as he does when his legs
hurt from standing too long
in the pen, then the pub,
and listens to him skip

the step of the stair
that creaks. *Son –*
she says sometimes
before opening her eyes
to night, holding her hand

out to the edge of the bed,
bidding the black cat, busy
stalking some smaller life
in the corner, to join her
in the last hour before light.

The first thing he doesn't forget

*'LMTX pill invented by Professor Claude Wischik at the University of Aberdeen
can slow the progression of Alzheimer's'*
  – The Times, May 2015

is where he put his glasses,
reaches for them on the top
of his head. And then that today
is his wife's birthday.
He can still taste breakfast,
the halved pink grapefruit
he carved into smaller sections
then ate before pouring
the juice from its scooped-out
hollow into his mouth,
like a boy drinking straight
from the carton. The last
of the yellow post-it notes
on the fridge says
Professor Claude Wischik,
a name he should memorise;
instead, he says it aloud
at the start of each Wischik day.
On his way out,
he grabs his keys
from the dish by the door.

The Unfinished House

after George Mackay Brown

What is a house but a borderline –
bodies we love huddled shoulder
to shoulder around a wooden table
waiting for a hot ladle of soup,
the buttered heel of bread.
A beaker of water sits between us,
the last drops refilled from the leaking
tap that keeps time against the sink
like a clock. Above our heads,
the roof holds off the sky, with its
chance of rain and its chance of sun,
while the warmth of the stove
draws us back, becomes a tether
to the stone floor under our feet.

Storm Light

In the absolute dark of storm this light shines,
blinks, shines again as if morse-coded,

faster than the speed of sound, a howl
from a child, the wind against glass panes.

The guttering comes clean off the tacked felt roof.
Everything pinned down in daylight is upended.

In the absolute dark of storm hold the flash
of the lighthouse beacon between your hands.

Watch it flicker like a firefly, on and off,
burning and at rest, its back anchored

against the warmth of your lifeline,
just waiting for the right moment to fly.

The Last Keeper

the Barns Ness Lighthouse becomes automated in 1986

When he lights this final lamp he knows
       it will be extinguished, that no beacon can burn

across sea or land for a lifetime; even
       daylight and darkness, no matter the season,

draw to a close. He polishes the silver and trims
       the wick for old times' sake, wanting things

to be right and true, though no one else will know.
       Then he keeps vigil, watching it burn through,

refuses food or water as if air is enough.
       He knows what this means, his last night,

this last light; he knows from here on out,
       he is the only one in danger of darkness.

Citizen

In my dream, it is always black and white: a line
                 of people waiting, the stone building,
fists of flyers, a glass door framed in steel.

An old woman takes my name, checks it
                 against her printout, her pencil slides
through the letters of the registered.

I wonder again if I've gotten it wrong.
                 In my dream she asks me to say it again,
Lotfi, spell it out, before turning me away.

In my dream, I push through the exit
                 and walk home in rain to a house
that isn't mine, in a country that isn't mine.

Moving

When I left the house, I wanted
        to leave a light on, not for us –
our sofas and beds turned on end
        and lined up like schoolchildren
on the last day before summer –
        but for our absence, the lack
of us in this space. Within hours
        children would run across
these floorboards, claim this room
        or another, let the back door
slam in the rush to explore. I left
        the paper angel we'd found
on the day we moved in just where
        it'd been, silver wings open,
hanging in the upstairs cupboard.
        But that wasn't enough; I wanted
a light left ablaze, like a candle
        in a cathedral, for the keeping
of vigil, for the passing
        of this one short night.

And this is how it begins

> though it never begins, but begins again –
the weight of a thumb, maybe, across an exposed
> collarbone, knowing the fingers will follow
one dragging after another, playing the hollow
> of body as if testing a new tune on the skin,
almost mindless, pianissimo, the slow march to rest
> at the base of the windpipe. Here, you touch
breath before you hear it. Here, you hold down
> the pulse rising against the bone.

And this is how it ends
> though it never ends, but begins again –
the weight of arm against arm, the perfect puzzle
> of hip and cradle of belly against rib,
how the sleep of the spent exposes the crown
> of head, as if offering it up to the loved
without a need for return. *Here, take my treasure.*
> Here, and not before, the body is light,
holds itself apart, the pulse slows into its coda
> and night falls, whatever the hour.

O Love!

after Al Muttanabbi (915-965)

Before morning, before daybreak in summer even, this helpless light. Behind closed eyes, behind a gate of sleep. Before birdsong, and the wind rousing the sun, before the clock remembers to tick, before the fox abandons the bins out front, this helpless light. Before an intake of breath, or the first morning coffee, black as tar, before the key in any lock in the building, before the day of the week, this helpless light. Nothing will hold it off, not the stars or the moon, the rush of tide or the silence of bell tower, not the shipping forecast or hunger, not the lark or the owl, the darkness or dawn, this helpless light.

Edward Thomas on His Last Night with Helen

Every minute is stretched by speech, or touch,
the sheer act of listening to snow fall. He says

I would like to know how I've failed you.
She denies him, asks his hopes for the children,

and, put on the spot, he can think of nothing
but happiness, whatever its form. Finally,

he is at a loss for words. When light arrives,
the children dress and go out into the snow,

laughing against the wind. He watches them,
holding her hand, before carrying his bag

up the hill. At the summit, as usual, he calls
a last *coo-ee*, listening for her soundless echo.

Keep

There, in the already strawed grass
of a long spring, the river beneath running
low, slipping its stream below the shoulder,
you leaned over as if to pluck the keys
you'd dropped somewhere en route
and brought up instead a posy
of primrose, cupping their dairy-butter
faces, telling me their name.

Here, each April I spot the pale primrose
in the shade of the trees behind the house,
bring a handful in and strip the table
bare, place them on the wood alone
and sugar them, the paintbrush washing
each waxy petal with crystals that glint
the spring light, making their honey-sweetness
stretch another year, a little longer.

The Hebridean Crab Apple

mysterious lonely apple tree on uninhabited Hebridean island baffles scientists

This, I understand: the instinct to cling,
at any cost, to the place you are rooted,
to see another season through, though
the others seed elsewhere. Even in this

sedentary act you push the limit: winter
becomes summer becomes winter
and you are steadfast on your crag,
your outcrop. No one knows the shape

of your limbs against a darkening sky;
you question the need to grow against
the wind. Despite what they say,
there's no mystery in simply holding on.

And what is home if not the choice –
over and over again – to stay?

ACKNOWLEDGEMENTS

The cover photograph is of Soghra Eskandari, my great-great-aunt, who was separated from her family during the closing of the Iran/ Azerbaijan border around 1917. The poem 'Khanoom' is in the voice of her mother.

I am grateful to the editors of the publications where earlier versions of some of these poems first appeared: *Acumen, Ambit, The Amsterdam Quarterly, Bella Caledonia, Beyond the Swelkie: A Collection of New Poems and Essays to Mark the Centenary of George Mackay Brown, Coast to Coast, CURA, Gutter, The Midwest Quarterly, Mind the Time, North, Ofi Press Magazine, Our Time is a Garden, Poetry for Change: A National Poetry Day Anthology, Rattle, The Reader, The Rialto, The Scotsman, Sprung: Poems from Spring Fling* and *Women on the Road.*

Some of these poems appeared in earlier forms in the House of Three Anthology published by House of Three Press and my pamphlet *Refuge*, published by Tapsalteerie Press.

'Maman Bozorg', 'To the Airport', 'Refuge' and 'On seeing Iran in the news, I want to say' appeared in German translation through UNESCO Cities of Literature, *Wunderhorn Verlag*.

'Maman Bozorg' and 'Refuge' were placed Runner Up and Highly Commended in the 2016 Wigtown Poetry Competition, respectively.

The two poems 'On seeing Iran in the news, I want to say' and 'The Wrong Person to Ask' were written in response respectively to the signing of, and then the withdrawal from, the Iran Nuclear Deal (Joint Comprehensive Plan of Action).

'Maman Bozorg' is about my Iranian grandmother's gift (a Catholic crucifix) to my American mother upon her arrival in Tehran.

'Two Grandmothers' is about the first meeting of my two Grandmothers, Marjorie Glasgow and Khanoom Nasreen Lotfi. Marjorie travelled to Tehran, just before the Iranian Revolution in 1978.

'The gun in its holster' was inspired by the sculpture *Landscape with Gun and Tree*, by Cornelia Parker, at Jupiter Artland, and was written in response to the shooting of Michael Brown in Ferguson Missouri in 2014.

'The Game' was written in response to the BBC's online inter-active game called *Syrian Journey: Choose your own escape route*, which claims to allows readers to experience the real choices of those fleeing their homeland.

'Packing for America' was first published by *Primers*/Nine Arches Press Competition.

The title of 'Shut out the Noise' is taken from President Obama's speech to the US Congress imploring US lawmakers to ratify the Iran nuclear deal: 'A nuclear-armed Iran is far more dangerous to Israel, to America, and to the world than an Iran that benefits from sanctions relief... and as members of Congress reflect...I urge them to set aside political concerns, shut out the noise.'

'Origin' was included in *Best Scottish Poems 2020*, and was commissioned as a part of the 12 Collective's response to Emma Hart's exhibition *BANGER* at the Fruitmarket Gallery, Edinburgh.

'Picture of Girl and Small Boy (Burij, Gaza, 2014)' was inspired by Finbar O'Reilly's photograph that appeared in *The Times* in August of 2014.

'Picture of Boy, Looking Away (Gaza, 2015)' was inspired by an image and the BBC news report of conditions in Gaza in July of 2015.

'Wishbone' was inspired in part by a film made for MAKING IT HOME, a project working with refugee and asylum-seeking women and other local women in Edinburgh.

'Khanoom' was written for my great-great grandmother Khanoom Eskandari, who was separated from her daughter Soghra during the closing of the Iran/Azerbaijan border in 1917. A photograph of Soghra, her daughter referred to in the poem, graces the cover of this book.

The sequence 'The End of the Road' was commissioned by Carlo Pirozzi and Davide Messina of the University of Edinburgh for a conference on the Myth of Europa.

The quotation at the end of 'Number 9 Cullipool' comes from George MacKenzie, a fisherman who lives in Cullipool, on the isle of Luing.

Williamina Fleming (1857–1911) was a Scottish astronomer who moved to the United States with her husband and was abandoned by him while pregnant. She took up work as a maid in the home of Professor Edward Charles Pickering, the director of the Harvard College Observatory. He is said to have shouted at his all-male team 'even my Scotch maid could do better!', and then proceeded to give her a job at the Observatory. Williamina went on to become one of the world's finest astronomers. She helped develop a common designation system for stars and catalogued thousands of stars and other astronomical phenomena. Among many others, Fleming is noted for her discovery of the Horsehead Nebula in 1888.

'What Work Is' is a poem written after the death of Philip Levine (1928-2015), Poet Laureate of the United States, who has both a poem and a collection by the same name.

'Out to Sea' won the National Galleries of Scotland *Inspired? Get*

Writing! Competition, and was inspired by John Bellany's painting *My Father* and the article 'The Luing of My Youth' (*Luing Newsletter*) by Angus Shaw, which includes the story of teen boys stealing a boat to try and row to Belnahua.

'The Trunk' was first broadcast on BBC Radio 4's *Something Understood*, and was written in response to *Away Being, Coming Home* – photographs of abandoned dwellings on the Hebrides – *Unmade Lewis* by Ian Paterson, still available online as a part of the Thrive Archive.

'The Unfinished House' was commissioned for *Beyond the Swelkie: A Collection of New Poems and Essays to Mark the Centenary of George Mackay Brown*, edited by Jim Mackintosh.

'Storm Light' and 'The Last Keeper' were written as part of my residency at the Coastword Festival, Dunbar.

'O Love' was written for Scottish PEN's *Al-Mutanabbi Street Starts Here*, in response to the poems of Iraqi poet Al-Mutanabbi (915–965).

Some of the details from 'Edward Thomas on His Last Night with Helen' were taken from the publication of an extract taken from *World Without End* by Helen Thomas (first published by William Heinemann Ltd, 1931; reprinted by Carcanet, 1987).

Thank you to the many people who have made this book possible by giving time and space and encouragement, often all three at once.

Thank you to Coley, my oldest friend, who reminded me that I was still a writer 12 years ago – this book would not exist without that early push of encouragement and the endless dialogue along the way. Thank you also to my dear friends Claire Urquhart and Valery Pollard, who have supported me in ways I cannot articulate here, but that have, among other things, allowed me to create this work. Many more friends have kept me sane and on the path of writing, especially Gabi who often held the fort when I was away writing, and Rachel, Beth, Tam, Esa, Krissy and Nics, each of whom contributed in their own way.

Thank you to my writing groups – the earliest Grangers (Finola, Anne, Helen, Tessa, Marie Thérèse, Jane and Jonathan), the women of the 12 Collective, and now my *only* poetry crit group (Francis, Hollie, Michael, Esa and Iain). I am the writer I am today because of you.

Thank you to Iain Matheson, for the exquisite time and attention, over many years, that he has given to my poems – I will always think of him as my first reader and be grateful. Thank you to Hannah Lavery and Heshani Sothiraj Eddleston for the many important conversations that have shaped my work, and for putting up with my crazy ideas. Thank you to Claire Askew for being an honest early reader of my poems, and to John Glenday for reading earlier versions of this book (and in each of our meetings since then, for reminding me that it needed to be out in the world when I was inclined to leave it in a drawer).

Thank you to my poetry teachers and especially Miriam Gamble, who pushed me to make my poetry cleaner, harder, less in the way of itself. More recently, the support and guidance of Mimi Khalvati – at once tender and firm – has made this collection what it is, and me a better writer.

Thank you also to the many organisations that have supported my writing across a decade in the form of awards, residencies and commissions: the James Berry Poetry Prize (Bloodaxe Books/NCLA), the National Library of Scotland, the Coastword Festival, Moniack Mhor, the Scottish Book Trust, the Scottish BPOC Network, the Scottish Poetry Library, StAnza, the University of Edinburgh, Enterprise Music Scotland, the Fruitmarket Gallery, the Talbot Rice Gallery, Jupiter Artland, Spring Fling and the Wigtown Book Festival, to name but a few. Thank you, too, to John Burnside for allowing me to reproduce his poem 'Prayer' as a fitting epigraph to this collection.

To Mom, Dad and Kamran: thank you for letting me tell our stories, for nodding along with such grace. Thank you to my 'Ohio' cousins Dana, Robin and Jess for being my cheerleaders from across the water, for reminding me who I am. To my Persian family, thank you for inspiring so many of the stories in this book; your lives are wound around and through my own, and I am grateful for our connection.

To my children Pete, Nasreen, Florence and John – thank you for allowing me to be your Mom first and a poet second, for being proud of me and always making me proud. And for listening to endless poems – most of them not mine! – around our kitchen table.

And thank you to Finn, for reminding me to live.